What Does It All Mean?

THOMAS NAGEL

What Does It All Mean?

A Very Short Introduction to Philosophy

OXFORD UNIVERSITY PRESS
New York   Oxford

Oxford University Press

Oxford   New York   Toronto
Delhi   Bombay   Calcutta   Madras   Karachi
Petaling Jaya   Singapore   Hong Kong   Tokyo
Nairobi   Dar es Salaam   Cape Town
Melbourne   Auckland

and associated companies in
Beirut   Berlin   Ibadan   Nicosia

Published by Oxford University Press, Inc.,
198 Madison Avenue, New York, New York 10016-4314

Oxford is a registered trademark of Oxford University Press

Library of Congress Cataloging-in-Publication Data
Nagel, Thomas.
What does it all mean?
1. Philosophy---Introductions.   I.   Title.
BD21.N24   1987   100   87-14316
ISBN-13 978-0-19-505292-3
ISBN-13 978-0-19-505216-9 (pbk)
ISBN-13 978-0-19-517437-3 (pbk in UK)

paper 50 49 48 47 46

Printed in the United States of America

Contents

Contents

What Does It All Mean?

1

Introduction

This book is a brief introduction to philosophy for people who don't know the first thing about the subject. People ordinarily study philosophy only when they go to college, and I suppose that most readers will be of college age or older. But that has nothing to do with the nature of the subject, and I would be very glad if the book were also of interest to intelligent high school students with a taste for abstract ideas and theoretical arguments—should any of them read it.

Our analytical capacities are often highly developed before we have learned a great deal about the world, and around the age of fourteen many people start to think about philosophical problems on their own—about what really exists, whether we can know anything, whether anything is really right or wrong, whether life has any meaning, whether death is the end. These problems have been written about for thousands of years, but the philosophical raw material comes directly from the world and our relation to it, not from writings of the past. That is why they come up again and again, in the heads of people who haven't read about them.

This is a direct introduction to nine philosophical problems, each of which can be understood in itself, without reference to the history of thought. I shall not discuss the great philosophical writings of the past or the cultural background of those writings. The center of philosophy lies in certain questions which the reflective human mind finds naturally puzzling, and the best way to begin the study of philosophy is to think about them directly. Once you've done that, you are in a better position to appreciate the work of others who have tried to solve the same problems.

Philosophy is different from science and from mathematics. Unlike science it doesn't rely on experiments or observation, but only on thought. And unlike mathematics it has no formal methods of proof. It is done just by asking questions, arguing, trying out ideas and thinking of possible arguments against them, and wondering how our concepts really work.

[4]

Introduction

The main concern of philosophy is to question and understand very common ideas that all of us use every day without thinking about them. A historian may ask what happened at some time in the past, but a philosopher will ask, "What is time?" A mathematician may investigate the relations among numbers, but a philosopher will ask, "What is a number?" A physicist will ask what atoms are made of or what explains gravity, but a philosopher will ask how we can know there is anything outside of our own minds. A psychologist may investigate how children learn a language, but a philosopher will ask, "What makes a word mean anything?" Anyone can ask whether it's wrong to sneak into a movie without paying, but a philosopher will ask, "What makes an action right or wrong?"

We couldn't get along in life without taking the ideas of time, number, knowledge, language, right and wrong for granted most of the time; but in philosophy we investigate those things themselves. The aim is to push our understanding of the world and ourselves a bit deeper. Obviously it isn't easy. The more basic the ideas you are trying to investigate, the fewer tools you have to work with. There isn't much you can assume or take for granted. So philosophy is a somewhat dizzying activity, and few of its results go unchallenged for long.

Since I believe the best way to learn about philosophy is to think about particular questions, I won't try to say more about its general nature. The nine problems we'll consider are these:

Knowledge of the world beyond our minds
Knowledge of minds other than our own
The relation between mind and brain
How language is possible
Whether we have free will
The basis of morality
What inequalities are unjust
The nature of death
The meaning of life

They are only a selection: there are many, many others.

What I say will reflect my own view of these problems and will not necessarily represent what most philosophers think. There probably isn't anything that most philosophers think about these questions anyway: philosophers disagree, and there are more than two sides to every philosophical question. My personal opinion is that most of these problems have not been solved, and that perhaps some of them never will be. But the object here is not to give answers—not even answers that I myself may think are right—but to introduce you to the problems in a very preliminary way so that you can worry about them yourself. Before learning a lot of philosophical theories it is better to get puzzled about the philosophical questions which those theories try to answer. And the best way to do that is to look at some possible solutions and see what is wrong with them. I'll try to leave the problems open, but even if I say what I think, you have no reason to believe it unless you find it convincing.

There are many excellent introductory texts that include selections from the great philosophers of the past and from more recent writings. This short book is not a substitute for that approach, but I hope it provides a first look at the subject that is as clear and direct as possible. If after reading it you decide to take a second look, you'll see how much more there is to say about these problems than I say here.

2

How Do We Know Anything?

If you think about it, the inside of your own mind is the only thing you can be sure of.

Whatever you believe—whether it's about the sun, moon, and stars, the house and neighborhood in which you live, history, science, other people, even the existence of your own body— is based on your experiences and thoughts, feelings and sense impressions. That's all you have to go on directly, whether you see the book in your hands, or feel the floor under your feet, or remember that George Washington was the first president of the United States, or that water is H_2O. Everything else is farther away from you than your inner experiences and thoughts, and reaches you only through them.

How Do We Know Anything?

Ordinarily you have no doubts about the existence of the floor under your feet, or the tree outside the window, or your own teeth. In fact most of the time you don't even think about the mental states that make you aware of those things: you seem to be aware of them directly. But how do you know they really exist?

If you try to argue that there must be an external physical world, because you wouldn't see buildings, people, or stars unless there were things out there that reflected or shed light into your eyes and caused your visual experiences, the reply is obvious: How do you know *that*? It's just another claim about the external world and your relation to it, and it has to be based on the evidence of your senses. *But you can rely on that specific evidence about how visual experiences are caused only if you can already rely in general on the contents of your mind to tell you about the external world. And that is exactly what has been called into question.* If you try to prove the reliability of your impressions by appealing to your impressions, you're arguing in a circle and won't get anywhere.

Would things seem any different to you if in fact all these things existed *only* in your mind—if everything you took to be the real world outside was just a giant dream or hallucination, from which you will never wake up? If it were like that, then of course you *couldn't* wake up, as you can from a dream, because it would mean there was no "real" world to wake up into. So it wouldn't be exactly like a normal dream or hallucination. As we usually think of dreams, they go on in the minds of people who are actually lying in a real bed in a real house, even if in the dream they are running away from a homicidal lawnmower through the streets of Kansas City. We also assume that normal dreams depend on what is happening in the dreamer's brain while he sleeps.

But couldn't all your experiences be like a giant dream with *no* external world outside it? How can you know that isn't what's going on? If all your experience were a dream with *nothing* outside, then any evidence you tried to use to prove to yourself that there was an outside world would just be part of the dream. If you knocked on the table or pinched yourself, you would hear the knock and feel the pinch, but that would be just one more thing going on inside your mind like everything else. It's no use: If you want to find out whether what's inside your mind is any guide to what's outside your mind, you can't depend on how things *seem*—from inside your mind—to give you the answer.

But what else is there to depend on? All your evidence about anything has to come through your mind—whether in the form of perception, the testimony of books and other people, or memory—and it is entirely consistent with everything you're aware of that *nothing at all* exists except the inside of your mind.

It's even possible that you don't have a body or a brain—since your beliefs about that come only through the evidence of your senses. You've never seen your brain—you just assume that everybody has one—but even if you had seen it, or thought you had, that would have been just another visual experience. Maybe *you*, the subject of experience, are the only thing that exists, and there is no physical world at all—no stars, no earth, no human bodies. Maybe there isn't even any space.

The most radical conclusion to draw from this would be that your mind *is* the only thing that exists. This view is called solipsism. It is a very lonely view, and not too many people have held it. As you can tell from that remark, I don't hold it myself. If I were a solipsist I probably wouldn't be writing this book, since I wouldn't believe there was anybody else to read it. On the other hand, perhaps I would write it to make my inner life more interesting, by including the impression of the appearance of the book in print, of other people reading it and telling me their reactions, and so forth. I might even get the impression of royalties, if I'm lucky.

Perhaps you are a solipsist: in that case you

will regard this book as a product of your own mind, coming into existence in your experience as you read it. Obviously nothing I can say can prove to you that I really exist, or that the book as a physical object exists.

On the other hand, to conclude that you are the only thing that exists is more than the evidence warrants. You can't *know* on the basis of what's in your mind that there's no world outside it. Perhaps the right conclusion is the more modest one that you don't know anything beyond your impressions and experiences. There may or may not be an external world, and if there is it may or may not be completely different from how it seems to you—there's no way for you to tell. This view is called skepticism about the external world.

An even stronger form of skepticism is possible. Similar arguments seem to show that you don't know anything even about your own past existence and experiences, since all you have to go on are the present contents of your mind, including memory impressions. If you can't be sure that the world outside your mind exists *now*, how can you be sure that you yourself existed *before* now? How do you know you didn't just come into existence a few minutes ago, complete with all your present memories? The only evidence that you couldn't have come into existence a few minutes ago depends on beliefs about how people and their memories are produced, which rely in turn on beliefs about what has happened in the past. But to rely on those beliefs to prove that you existed in the past would again be to argue in a circle. You would be assuming the reality of the past to prove the reality of the past.

It seems that you are stuck with nothing you can be sure of except the contents of your own mind at the present moment. And it seems that anything you try to do to argue your way out of this predicament will fail, because the argument will have to assume what you are trying to prove—the existence of the external world beyond your mind.

Suppose, for instance, you argue that there must be an external world, because it is incredible that you should be having all these experiences without there being *some* explanation in terms of external causes. The skeptic can make two replies. First, even if there are external causes, how can you tell from the contents of your experience what those causes are like? You've never observed any of them directly. Second, what is the basis of your idea that everything has to have an explanation? It's true that in your normal, nonphilosophical conception of the world, processes like those which go on in your mind are caused, at least in part, by other things outside them. But you can't assume that this is true if what you're trying to figure out is how you know *anything* about the world outside your mind. And there is no way to prove such a principle just by looking at what's *inside* your mind. However plausible the principle may seem to you, what reason do you have to believe that it applies to the world?

Science won't help us with this problem either, though it might seem to. In ordinary scientific thinking, we rely on general principles of explanation to pass from the way the world first seems to us to a different conception of what it is really like. We try to explain the appearances in terms of a theory that describes the reality behind them, a reality that we can't observe directly. That is how physics and chemistry conclude that all the things we see around us are composed of invisibly small atoms. Could we argue that the general belief in the external world has the same kind of scientific backing as the belief in atoms?

The skeptic's answer is that the process of scientific reasoning raises the same skeptical problem we have been considering all along: Science is just as vulnerable as perception. How can we know that the world outside our minds corresponds to our ideas of what would be a good theoretical explanation of our observations? If we can't establish the reliability of our sense experiences in relation to the external world, there's no reason to think we can rely on our scientific theories either.

There is another very different response to the problem. Some would argue that radical skepticism of the kind I have been talking about is meaningless, because the idea of an external reality that *no one* could ever discover is meaningless. The argument is that a dream, for instance, has to be something from which you *can* wake up to discover that you have been asleep; a hallucination has to be something which others (or you later) *can* see is not really there. Impressions and appearances that do not correspond to reality must be contrasted with others that *do* correspond to reality, or else the contrast between appearance and reality is meaningless.

According to this view, the idea of a dream from which you can never wake up is not the idea of a dream at all: it is the idea of *reality*— the real world in which you live. Our idea of the things that exist is just our idea of what we can observe. (This view is sometimes called verificationism.) Sometimes our observations are mistaken, but that means they can be corrected by other observations— as when you wake up from a dream or discover that what you thought was

[15]

a snake was just a shadow on the grass. But without some possibility of a correct view of how things are (either yours or someone else's), the thought that your impressions of the world are not true is meaningless.

If this is right, then the skeptic is kidding himself if he thinks he can imagine that the only thing that exists is his own mind. He is kidding himself, because it couldn't be true that the physical world doesn't really exist, unless somebody could *observe* that it doesn't exist. And what the skeptic is trying to imagine is precisely that there *is* no one to observe that or anything else—except of course the skeptic himself, and all he can observe is the inside of his own mind. So solipsism is meaningless. It tries to subtract the external world from the totality of my impressions; but it fails, because if the external world is subtracted, they stop being mere impressions, and become instead perceptions of reality.

Is this argument against solipsism and skepticism any good? Not unless reality can be defined as what we can observe. But are we really unable to understand the idea of a real world, or a fact about reality, that can't be observed by anyone, human or otherwise?

The skeptic will claim that if there is an external world, the things in it are observable because they exist, and not the other way around: that existence isn't the same thing as observability. And although we get the idea of dreams and hallucinations from cases where we think we *can* observe the contrast between our experiences and reality, it certainly seems as if the same idea can be extended to cases where the reality is not observable.

If that is right, it seems to follow that it is not meaningless to think that the world might consist of nothing but the inside of your mind, though neither you nor anyone else could find out that this was true. And if this is not meaningless, but is a possibility you must consider, there seems no way to prove that it is false, without arguing in a circle. So there may be no way out of the cage of your own mind. This is sometimes called the egocentric predicament.

And yet, after all this has been said, I have to admit it is practically impossible to believe seriously that all the things in the world around you might not really exist. Our acceptance of the external world is instinctive and powerful: we cannot just get rid of it by philosophical arguments. Not only do we go on acting *as if* other people and things exist: we *believe* that they do, even after we've gone through the arguments which appear to show we have no grounds for this belief. (We may have grounds, within the overall system of our beliefs about the world, for more particular beliefs about the existence of particular things: like a mouse in the breadbox, for example. But that is different. It assumes the existence of the external world.)

If a belief in the world outside our minds comes so naturally to us, perhaps we don't need grounds for it. We can just let it be and hope that we're right. And that in fact is what most people do after giving up the attempt to prove it: even if they can't give reasons against skepticism, they can't live with it either. But this means that we hold on to most of our ordinary beliefs about the world in face of the fact that (a) they might be completely false, and (b) we have no basis for ruling out that possibility.

We are left then with three questions:

1. Is it a meaningful possibility that the inside of your mind is the only thing that exists—or that even if there is a world outside your mind, it is totally unlike what you believe it to be?
2. If these things are possible, do you have any way of proving to yourself that they are not actually true?
3. If you can't prove that anything exists outside your own mind, is it all right to go on believing in the external world anyway?

3

Other Minds

There is one special kind of skepticism which continues to be a problem even if you assume that your mind is not the only thing there is— that the physical world you seem to see and feel around you, including your own body, really exists. That is skepticism about the nature or even existence of minds or experiences other than your own.

How much do you really know about what goes on in anyone else's mind? Clearly you observe only the bodies of other creatures, including people. You watch what they do, listen to what they say and to the other sounds they make, and see how they respond to their environment—what things attract them and what things repel them, what they eat, and so forth. You can also cut open other creatures and look at their physical insides, and perhaps compare their anatomy with yours.

But none of this will give you direct access to their experiences, thoughts, and feelings. The only experiences you can actually have are your own: if you believe anything about the mental lives of others, it is on the basis of observing their physical construction and behavior.

To take a simple example, how do you know, when you and a friend are eating chocolate ice cream, whether it tastes the same to him as it tastes to you? You can try a taste of his ice cream, but if it tastes the same as yours, that only means it tastes the same *to you*: you haven't experienced the way it tastes *to him*. There seems to be no way to compare the two flavor experiences directly.

Well, you might say that since you're both human beings, and you can both distinguish among flavors of ice cream—for example you can both tell the difference between chocolate and vanilla with your eyes closed—it's likely that your flavor experiences are similar. But how do you know *that*? The only connection you've ever observed between a type of ice cream and a flavor is in your own case; so what reason do you have to think that similar correlations hold for other human beings? Why isn't it just as consistent with all the evidence that chocolate tastes to him the way vanilla tastes to you, and vice versa?

The same question could be asked about other kinds of experience. How do you know that red things don't look to your friend the way yellow things look to you? Of course if you ask him how a fire engine looks, he'll say it looks red, like blood, and not yellow, like a dandelion; but that's because he, like you, uses the word "red" for the color that blood and fire engines look to him, *whatever* it is. Maybe it's what you call yellow, or what you call blue, or maybe it's a color experience you've never had, and can't even imagine.

To deny this, you have to appeal to an assumption that flavor and color experiences are uniformly correlated with certain physical stimulations of the sense organs, whoever undergoes them. But the skeptic would say you have no evidence for that assumption, and because of the kind of assumption it is, you *couldn't* have any evidence for it. All you can observe is the correlation in your own case.

Faced with this argument, you might first concede that there is some uncertainty here. The correlation between stimulus and experience may not be exactly the same from one person to another: there may be slight shades of difference between two people's color or flavor experience of the same type of ice cream. In fact, since people are physically different from one another, this wouldn't be surprising. But, you might say,

[21]

the difference in experience can't be too radical, or else we'd be able to tell. For instance, chocolate ice cream couldn't taste to your friend the way a lemon tastes to you, otherwise his mouth would pucker up when he ate it.

But notice that this claim assumes another correlation from one person to another: a correlation between inner experience and certain kinds of observable reaction. And the same question arises about that. You've observed the connection between puckering of the mouth and the taste you call sour only in your own case: how do you know it exists in other people? Maybe what makes your friend's mouth pucker up is an experience like the one you get from eating oatmeal.

If we go on pressing these kinds of questions relentlessly enough, we will move from a mild and harmless skepticism about whether chocolate ice cream tastes exactly the same to you and to your friend, to a much more radical skepticism about whether there is *any* similarity between your experiences and his. How do you know that when he puts something in his mouth he even has an experience of the kind that you would call a *flavor*? For all you know, it could be something you would call a sound—or maybe it's unlike anything you've ever experienced, or could imagine.

If we continue on this path, it leads finally to the most radical skepticism of all about other minds. How do you even know that your friend is conscious? How do you know that there are *any minds at all* besides your own?

The only example you've ever directly observed of a correlation between mind, behavior, anatomy, and physical circumstances is yourself. Even if other people and animals had no experiences whatever, no mental inner life of any kind, but were just elaborate biological machines, they would look just the same to you. So how do you know that's not what they are? How do you know that the beings around you aren't all mindless robots? You've never seen into their minds—you couldn't—and their physical behavior could all be produced by purely physical causes. Maybe your relatives, your neighbors, your cat and your dog have *no inner experiences whatever*. If they don't, there is no way you could ever find it out.

You can't even appeal to the evidence of their behavior, including what they say—because that assumes that in them outer behavior is connected with inner experience as it is in you; and that's just what you don't know.

To consider the possibility that none of the people around you may be conscious produces an uncanny feeling. On the one hand it seems conceivable, and no evidence you could possibly have can rule it out decisively. On the other hand it is something you can't *really* believe is possible: your conviction that there are minds in those bodies, sight behind those eyes, hearing in those ears, etc., is instinctive. But if its power comes from instinct, is it really knowledge? Once you admit the *possibility* that the belief in other minds is mistaken, don't you need something more reliable to justify holding on to it?

There is another side to this question, which goes completely in the opposite direction.

Ordinarily we believe that other human beings are conscious, and almost everyone believes that other mammals and birds are conscious too. But people differ over whether fish are conscious, or insects, worms, and jellyfish. They are still more doubtful about whether one-celled animals like amoebae and paramecia have conscious experiences, even though such creatures react conspicuously to stimuli of various kinds. Most people believe that plants aren't conscious; and almost no one believes that rocks are conscious, or kleenex, or automobiles, or mountain lakes, or cigarettes. And to take another biological example, most of us would say, if we thought about it, that the individual cells of which our bodies are composed do not have any conscious experiences.

How do we know all these things? How do you know that when you cut a branch off a tree it doesn't hurt the tree—only it can't express its pain because it can't move? (Or maybe it *loves* having its branches pruned.) How do you know that the muscle cells in your heart don't feel pain or excitement when you run up a flight of stairs? How do you know that a kleenex doesn't feel anything when you blow your nose into it?

And what about computers? Suppose computers are developed to the point where they can be used to control robots that look on the outside like dogs, respond in complicated ways to the environment, and behave in many ways just like dogs, though they are just a mass of circuitry and silicon chips on the inside? Would we have any way of knowing whether such machines were conscious?

These cases are different from one another, of course. If a thing is incapable of movement, it can't give any behavioral evidence of feeling or perception. And if it isn't a natural organism, it is radically different from us in internal constitution. But what grounds do we have for thinking that only things that behave like us to some degree and that have an observable physical structure roughly like ours are capable of having experiences of *any* kind? Perhaps trees feel things in a way totally different from us, but we have no way of finding out about it, because we have no way of discovering the correlations between experience and observable manifestations or physical conditions in their case. We could discover such correlations only if we could observe both the experiences and the external manifestations together: but there is no way we can observe the experiences directly, except in our own case. And for the same reason there is no way we could observe the *absence* of any experiences, and consequently the absence of any such correlations, in any other case. You can't tell that a tree has *no* experience, by looking inside it, any more than you can tell that a worm *has* experience, by looking inside it.

So the question is: what can you really know about the conscious life in this world beyond the fact that you yourself have a conscious mind? Is it possible that there might be much less conscious life than you assume (none except yours), or much more (even in things you assume to be unconscious)?

4

The Mind-Body Problem

Let's forget about skepticism, and assume the physical world exists, including your body and your brain; and let's put aside our skepticism about other minds. I'll assume you're conscious if you assume I am. Now what might be the relation between consciousness and the brain?

Everybody knows that what happens in consciousness depends on what happens to the body. If you stub your toe it hurts. If you close your eyes you can't see what's in front of you. If you bite into a Hershey bar you taste chocolate. If someone conks you on the head you pass out.

The evidence shows that for anything to happen in your mind or consciousness, something has to happen in your brain. (You wouldn't feel any pain from stubbing your toe if the nerves in your leg and spine didn't carry impulses from the toe to your brain.) We don't know what happens in the brain when you think, "I wonder whether I have time to get a haircut this afternoon." But we're pretty sure something does—something involving chemical and electrical changes in the billions of nerve cells that your brain is made of.

In some cases, we know how the brain affects the mind and how the mind affects the brain. We know, for instance, that the stimulation of certain brain cells near the back of the head produces visual experiences. And we know that when you decide to help yourself to another piece of cake, certain other brain cells send out impulses to the muscles in your arm. We don't know many of the details, but it is clear that there are complex relations between what happens in your mind and the physical processes that go on in your brain. So far, all of this belongs to science, not philosophy.

But there is also a philosophical question about the relation between mind and brain, and it is this: Is your mind something different from your brain, though connected to it, or *is* it your brain? Are your thoughts, feelings, perceptions, sensations, and wishes things that happen *in addition* to all the physical processes in your brain, or are they themselves some of those physical processes?

[28]

What happens, for instance, when you bite into a chocolate bar? The chocolate melts on your tongue and causes chemical changes in your taste buds; the taste buds send some electrical impulses along the nerves leading from your tongue to your brain, and when those impulses reach the brain they produce further physical changes there; finally, *you taste the taste of chocolate*. What is *that*? Could it just *be* a physical event in some of your brain cells, or does it have to be something of a completely different kind?

If a scientist took off the top of your skull and looked into your brain while you were eating the chocolate bar, all he would see is a grey mass of neurons. If he used instruments to measure what was happening inside, he would detect complicated physical processes of many different kinds. But would he find the taste of chocolate?

It seems as if he couldn't find it in your brain, because your experience of tasting chocolate is locked inside your mind in a way that makes it unobservable by anyone else—even if he opens up your skull and looks inside your brain. Your experiences are inside your mind with a *kind of insideness* that is different from the way that your brain is inside your head. Someone else can open up your head and see what's inside, but they can't cut open your mind and look into it— at least not in the same way.

It's not just that the taste of chocolate is a flavor and therefore can't be seen. Suppose a scientist were crazy enough to try to observe your experience of tasting chocolate by *licking* your brain while you ate a chocolate bar. First of all, your brain probably wouldn't taste like chocolate to him at all. But even if it did, he wouldn't have succeeded in getting into your mind and observing *your* experience of tasting chocolate. He would just have discovered, oddly enough, that when you taste chocolate, your brain changes so that it tastes like chocolate to other people. He would have his taste of chocolate and you would have yours.

If what happens in your experience is inside your mind in a way in which what happens in your brain is not, it looks as though your experiences and other mental states can't just be physical states of your brain. There has to be more to you than your body with its humming nervous system.

One possible conclusion is that there has to be a soul, attached to your body in some way which allows them to interact. If that's true, then you are made up of two very different things: a complex physical organism, and a soul which is purely mental. (This view is called dualism, for obvious reasons.)

But many people think that belief in a soul is old-fashioned and unscientific. Everything else in the world is made of physical matter—different combinations of the same chemical elements. Why shouldn't we be? Our bodies grow by a complex physical process from the single cell produced by the joining of sperm and egg at conception. Ordinary matter is added gradually in such a way that the cell turns into a baby, with arms, legs, eyes, ears, and a brain, able to move and feel and see, and eventually to talk and think. Some people believe that this complex physical system is sufficient by itself to give rise to mental life. Why shouldn't it be? Anyway, how can mere philosophical argument show that it isn't? Philosophy can't tell us what stars or diamonds are made of, so how can it tell us what people are or aren't made of?

The view that people consist of nothing but physical matter, and that their mental states are physical states of their brains, is called physicalism (or sometimes materialism). Physicalists don't have a specific theory of what process in the brain can be identified as the experience of tasting chocolate, for instance. But they believe that mental states *are* just states of the brain, and that there's no philosophical reason to think they can't be. The details will have to be discovered by science.

The idea is that we might discover that experiences are really brain processes just as we have discovered that other familiar things have a real nature that we couldn't have guessed until it was revealed by scientific investigation. For instance, it turns out that diamonds are composed of carbon, the same material as coal: the atoms are just differently arranged. And water, as we all know, is composed of hydrogen and oxygen, even though those two elements are nothing like water when taken by themselves.

So while it might seem surprising that the experience of tasting chocolate could be nothing but a complicated physical event in your brain, it would be no stranger than lots of things that have been discovered about the real nature of ordinary objects and processes. Scientists have discovered what light is, how plants grow, how muscles move—it is only a matter of time before they discover the biological nature of the mind. That's what physicalists think.

A dualist would reply that those other things are different. When we discover the chemical composition of water, for instance, we are dealing with something that is clearly out there in the physical world—something we can all see and touch. When we find out that it's made up of hydrogen and oxygen atoms, we're just breaking down an external physical substance into smaller physical parts. It is an essential feature of this kind of analysis that we are not giving a chemical breakdown of the way water *looks*, *feels*, and *tastes* to us. Those things go on in our inner experience, not in the water that we have broken down into atoms. The physical or chemical analysis of water leaves them aside.

But to discover that tasting chocolate was really just a brain process, we would have to analyze something mental—not an externally observed physical substance but an inner taste sensation—in terms of parts that are physical. And there is no way that a large number of physical events in the brain, however complicated, could be the parts out of which a taste sensation was composed. A physical whole can be analyzed into smaller physical parts, but a mental process can't be. Physical parts just can't add up to a mental whole.

There is another possible view which is different from both dualism and physicalism. Dualism is the view that you consist of a body plus a soul, and that your mental life goes on in your soul. Physicalism is the view that your mental life consists of physical processes in your brain. But another possibility is that your mental life goes on in your brain, yet that all those experiences, feelings, thoughts, and desires are not *physical* processes in your brain. This would mean that the grey mass of billions of nerve cells in your skull is *not just a physical object*. It has lots of physical properties—great quantities of chemical and electrical activity go on in it—but it has *mental* processes going on in it as well.

The view that the brain is the seat of consciousness, but that its conscious states are not just physical states, is called dual aspect theory. It is called that because it means that when you bite into a chocolate bar, this produces in your brain a state or process with two aspects: a physical aspect involving various chemical and electrical changes, and a mental aspect—the flavor experience of chocolate. When this process occurs, a scientist looking into your brain will be able to observe the physical aspect, but you yourself will undergo, from the inside, the mental aspect: you will have the sensation of tasting chocolate. If this were true, your brain itself would have an inside that could not be reached by an outside observer even if he cut it open. It would feel, or taste, a certain way to you to have that process going on in your brain.

We could express this view by saying that you are not a body plus a soul—that you are just a body, but your body, or at least your brain, is not just a physical system. It is an object with both physical and mental aspects: it can be dissected, but it also has the kind of inside that can't be exposed by dissection. There's something it's like from the inside to taste chocolate because there's something it's like from the inside to have your brain in the condition that is produced when you eat a chocolate bar.

Physicalists believe that nothing exists but the physical world that can be studied by science: the world of objective reality. But then they have to find room somehow for feelings, desires, thoughts, and experiences—for you and me— in such a world.

One theory offered in defense of physicalism is that the mental nature of your mental states consists in their relations to things that cause them and things they cause. For instance, when you stub your toe and feel pain, the pain is something going on in your brain. But its pain- fulness is not just the sum of its physical char- acteristics, and it is not some mysterious non- physical property either. Rather, what makes it a pain is that it is the kind of state of your brain that is usually caused by injury, and that usually causes you to yell and hop around and avoid the thing that caused the injury. And that could be a purely physical state of your brain.

But that doesn't seem enough to make some- thing a pain. It's true that pains are caused by injury, and they do make you hop and yell. But they also *feel* a certain way, and that seems to be something different from all their relations to causes and effects, as well as all the physical properties they may have—if they are in fact events in your brain. I myself believe that this inner aspect of pain and other conscious experiences cannot be adequately analyzed in terms of any system of causal relations to physical stimuli and behavior, however complicated.

There seem to be two very different kinds of things going on in the world: the things that belong to physical reality, which many different people can observe from the outside, and those other things that belong to mental reality, which each of us experiences from the inside in his own case. This isn't true only of human beings: dogs and cats and horses and birds seem to be conscious, and fish and ants and beetles probably are too. Who knows where it stops?

We won't have an adequate general conception of the world until we can explain how, when a lot of physical elements are put together in the right way, they form not just a functioning biological organism but a conscious being. If consciousness itself could be identified with some kind of physical state, the way would be open for a unified physical theory of mind and body, and therefore perhaps for a unified physical theory of the universe. But the reasons against a purely physical theory of consciousness are strong enough to make it seem likely that a physical theory of the whole of reality is impossible. Physical science has progressed by leaving the mind out of what it tries to explain, but there may be more to the world than can be understood by physical science.

5

The Meaning of Words

How can a word—a noise or a set of marks on paper—*mean* something? There are some words, like "bang" or "whisper," which sound a bit like what they refer to, but usually there is no resemblance between a name and the thing it is the name of. The relation in general must be something entirely different.

There are many types of words: some of them name people or things, others name qualities or activities, others refer to relations between things or events, others name numbers, places, or times, and some, like "and" and "of," have meaning only because they contribute to the meaning of larger statements or questions in which they appear as parts. In fact all words do their real work in this way: their meaning is really something they contribute to the meaning of sentences or statements. Words are mostly used in talking and writing, rather than just as labels.

However, taking that as understood, let us ask how a word can have a meaning. Some words can be defined in terms of other words: "square" for example means "four-sided equilateral equiangular plane figure." And most of the terms in that definition can also be defined. But definitions can't be the basis of meaning for all words, or we'd go forever in a circle. Eventually we must get to some words which have meaning directly.

Take the word "tobacco," which may seem like an easy example. It refers to a kind of plant whose Latin name most of us don't know, and whose leaves are used to make cigars and cigarettes. All of us have seen and smelled tobacco, but the word as you use it refers not just to the samples of the stuff that you have seen, or that is around you when you use the word, but to all examples of it, whether or not you know of their existence. You may have learned the word by being shown some samples, but you won't understand it if you think it is just the name of those samples.

So if you say, "I wonder if more tobacco was smoked in China last year than in the entire

Western hemisphere," you have asked a meaningful question, and it has an answer, even if you can't find it out. But the meaning of the question, and its answer, depend on the fact that when you use the word "tobacco," it refers to every example of the substance in the world— throughout all past and future time, in fact—to every cigarette smoked in China last year, to every cigar smoked in Cuba, and so forth. The other words in the sentence limit the reference to particular times and places, but the word "tobacco" can be used to ask such a question only because it has this enormous but special reach, beyond all your experience to every sample of a certain kind of stuff.

How does the word do that? How can a mere *noise* or *scribble* reach that far? Not, obviously, because of its sound or look. And not because of the relatively small number of examples of tobacco that you've encountered, and that have been in the same room when you have uttered or heard or read the word. There's something else going on, and it is something general, which applies to everyone's use of the word. You and I, who have never met and have encountered different samples of tobacco, use the word with the same meaning. If we both use the word to ask the question about China and the Western hemisphere, it is the same question, and the answer is the same. Further, a speaker of Chinese can ask the same question, using the Chinese word with the same meaning. Whatever relation the word "tobacco" has to the stuff itself, other words can have as well.

This very naturally suggests that the relation of the word "tobacco" to all those plants, cigarettes, and cigars in the past, present, and future, is indirect. The word as you use it has something else behind it—a concept or idea or thought—which somehow reaches out to all the tobacco in the universe. This, however, raises new problems.

First, what kind of thing is this middleman? Is it in your mind, or is it something outside your mind that you somehow latch onto? It would seem to have to be something that you and I and a speaker of Chinese can all latch onto, in order to mean the same thing by our words for tobacco. But how, with our very different experiences of the word and the plant, do we do that? Isn't this just as hard to explain as our all being able to refer to the same enormous and widespread amount of *stuff* by our different uses of the word or words? Isn't there just as much of a problem about how the word means the idea or concept (whatever that is) as there was before about how the word means the plant or substance?

Not only that, but there's also a problem about how this idea or concept is related to all the samples of actual tobacco. What kind of thing is it that it can have this exclusive connection with tobacco and nothing else? It looks as though we've just added to the problem. In trying to explain the relation between the word "tobacco" and tobacco by interposing between them the *idea* or *concept* of tobacco, we've just created the further need to explain the relations between the word and the idea, and between the idea and the stuff.

With or without the concept or idea, the problem seems to be that very particular sounds, marks, and examples are involved in each person's use of a word, but the word applies to something universal, which other particular speakers can also mean by that word or other words in other languages. How can anything as particular as the noise I make when I say "tobacco" mean something so general that I can use it to say, "I bet people will be smoking tobacco on Mars 200 years from now."

You might think that the universal element is provided by something we all have in our minds when we use the word. But what do we all have in our minds? Consciously, at least, I don't need anything more than the word itself in my mind to think, "Tobacco is getting more expensive every year." Still, I certainly may have an image of some sort in my mind when I use the word: perhaps of a plant, or of some dried leaves, or of the inside of a cigarette. Still, this will not help to explain the generality of the meaning of the word, because any such image will be a *particular* image. It will be an image of the appearance or smell of a particular sample of tobacco; and how is *that* supposed to encompass all actual and possible examples of tobacco? Also, even if you have a certain picture in your mind when you hear or use the word "tobacco," every other person will probably have a different picture; yet that does not prevent us all from using the word with the same meaning.

The mystery of meaning is that it doesn't seem to be located anywhere—not in the word, not in the mind, not in a separate concept or idea hovering between the word, the mind, and the things we are talking about. And yet we use language all the time, and it enables us to think complicated thoughts which span great reaches of time and space. You can talk about how many people in Okinawa are over five feet tall, or whether there is life in other galaxies, and the little noises you make will be sentences which are true or false in virtue of complicated facts about far away things that you will probably never encounter directly.

You may think I have been making too much of the universal reach of language. In ordinary life, most of the statements and thoughts we use language for are much more local and particular. If I say "Pass the salt," and you pass me the salt, this doesn't have to involve any universal meaning of the word "salt," of the kind that's present when we ask, "How long ago in the history of our galaxy was salt first formed out of sodium and chlorine?" Words are often used simply as tools in the relations between people. On a sign in a bus station you see the little figure with the skirt, and an arrow, and you know that's the way to the ladies' room. Isn't most of language just a system of signals and responses like that?

Well, perhaps some of it is, and perhaps that's how we start to learn to use words: "Daddy," "Mommy," "No," "All gone." But it doesn't stop there, and it's not clear how the simple transactions possible using one or two words at a time can help us to understand the use of language to describe and misdescribe the world far beyond our present neighborhood It seems more likely, in fact, that the use of language for much larger purposes shows us something about what is going on when we use it on a smaller scale.

A statement like, "There's salt on the table,"

means the same whether it's said for practical reasons during lunch, or as part of the description of a situation distant in space and time, or merely as a hypothetical description of an imaginary possibility. It means the same whether it is true or false, and whether or not the speaker or hearer know if it's true or false. Whatever is going on in the ordinary, practical case must be something general enough also to explain these other, quite different cases where it means the same thing.

It is of course important that language is a social phenomenon. Each person doesn't make it up for himself. When as children we learn a language, we get plugged into an already existing system, in which millions of people have been using the same words to talk to one another for centuries. My use of the word "tobacco" doesn't have a meaning just on its own, but rather as part of the much wider use of that word in English. (Even if I were to adopt a private code, in which I used the word "blibble" to mean tobacco, I'd do it by defining "blibble" to myself in terms of the common word "tobacco.") We still have to explain how my use of the word gets its content from all those other uses, most of which I don't know about—but putting my words into this larger context may seem to help explain their universal meaning.

But this doesn't solve the problem. When I use the word, it may have its meaning as part of the English language, but how does the use of the word by all those other speakers of English give it its universal range, well beyond all the situations in which it is actually used? The problem of the relation of language to the world is not so different whether we are talking about one sentence or billions. The meaning of a word contains all its possible uses, true and false, not only its actual ones, and the actual uses are only a tiny fraction of the possible ones.

We are small finite creatures, but meaning enables us with the help of sounds or marks on paper to grasp the whole world and many things in it, and even to invent things that do not exist and perhaps never will. The problem is to explain how this is possible: How does anything we say or write mean anything—including all the words in this book?

6

Free Will

Suppose you're going through a cafeteria line and when you come to the desserts, you hesitate between a peach and a big wedge of chocolate cake with creamy icing. The cake looks good, but you know it's fattening. Still, you take it and eat it with pleasure. The next day you look in the mirror or get on the scale and think, "I wish I hadn't eaten that chocolate cake. I could have had a peach instead."

"I could have had a peach instead." What does that mean, and is it true?

Peaches were available when you went through the cafeteria line: you had the *opportunity* to take a peach instead. But that isn't all you mean. You mean you could have *taken* the peach instead of the cake. You could have *done* something different from what you actually did. Before you made up your mind, it was open whether you would take fruit or cake, and it was only your choice that decided which it would be.

Is that it? When you say, "I could have had a peach instead," do you mean that it depended only on your choice? You chose chocolate cake, so that's what you had, but *if* you had chosen the peach, you would have had that.

This still doesn't seem to be enough. You don't mean only that *if* you had chosen the peach, you would have had it. When you say, "I could have had a peach instead," you also mean that you *could have chosen* it—no "ifs" about it. But what does that mean?

It can't be explained by pointing out other occasions when you *have* chosen fruit. And it can't be explained by saying that if you had thought about it harder, or if a friend had been with you who eats like a bird, you *would* have chosen it. What you are saying is that you could have chosen a peach instead of chocolate cake *just then, as things actually were*. You think you could have chosen a peach even if everything else had been exactly the same as it was up to the point when you in fact chose chocolate cake. The only difference would have been that instead of thinking, "Oh well," and reaching for the cake, you would have thought, "Better not," and reached for the peach.

This is an idea of "can" or "could have" which we apply only to people (and maybe some animals). When we say, "The car could have climbed to the top of the hill," we mean the car had enough power to reach the top of the hill *if* someone drove it there. We don't mean that on an occasion when it was parked at the bottom of the hill, the car could have just taken off and climbed to the top, instead of continuing to sit there. Something else would have had to happen differently first, like a person getting in and starting the motor. But when it comes to people, we seem to think that they can do various things they don't actually do, *just like that*, without anything else happening differently first. What does this mean?

Part of what it means may be this: Nothing up to the point at which you choose determines irrevocably what your choice will be. It remains an *open possibility* that you will choose a peach until the moment when you actually choose chocolate cake. It isn't determined in advance.

Some things that happen *are* determined in advance. For instance, it seems to be determined in advance that the sun will rise tomorrow at a certain hour. It is not an open possibility that tomorrow the sun won't rise and night will just continue. That is not possible because it could happen only if the earth stopped rotating, or the sun stopped existing, and there is nothing going on in our galaxy which might make either of those things happen. The earth will continue rotating unless it is stopped, and tomorrow morning its rotation will bring us back around to face inward in the solar system, toward the sun, instead of outward, away from it. If there is no possibility that the earth will stop or that the sun won't be there, there is no possibility that the sun won't rise tomorrow.

When you say you could have had a peach instead of chocolate cake, part of what you mean may be that it wasn't determined in advance what you would do, as it *is* determined in advance that the sun will rise tomorrow. There were no processes or forces at work before you made your choice that made it inevitable that you would choose chocolate cake.

That may not be all you mean, but it seems to be at least part of what you mean. For if it was really determined in advance that you would choose cake, how could it also be true that you could have chosen fruit? It would be true that nothing would have prevented you from having a peach if you had chosen it instead of cake. But these *ifs* are not the same as saying you could have chosen a peach, period. You couldn't have chosen it unless the possibility remained open until you closed it off by choosing cake.

Some people have thought that it is never possible for us to do anything different from what we actually do, in this absolute sense. They acknowledge that what we do depends on our choices, decisions, and wants, and that we make different choices in different circumstances: we're not like the earth rotating on its axis with monotonous regularity. But the claim is that, in each case, the circumstances that exist before we act determine our actions and make them inevitable. The sum total of a person's experiences, desires and knowledge, his hereditary constitution, the social circumstances and the nature of the choice facing him, together with other factors that we may not know about, all combine to make a particular action in the circumstances inevitable.

This view is called determinism. The idea is not that we can know all the laws of the universe and use them to *predict* what will happen. First of all, we can't know all the complex circumstances that affect a human choice. Secondly, even when we do learn something about the circumstances, and try to make a prediction, that is itself a *change* in the circumstances, which may change the predicted result. But predictability isn't the point. The hypothesis is that there *are* laws of nature, like those that govern the movement of the planets, which govern everything that happens in the world—and that in accordance with those laws, the circumstances before an action determine that it will happen, and rule out any other possibility.

If that is true, then even while you were making up your mind about dessert, it was already determined by the many factors working on you and in you that you would choose cake. You *couldn't* have chosen the peach, even though you thought you could: the process of decision is just the working out of the determined result inside your mind.

If determinism is true for everything that happens, it was already determined before you were born that you would choose cake. Your choice was determined by the situation immediately before, and *that* situation was determined by the situation before *it*, and so on as far back as you want to go.

Even if determinism isn't true for everything that happens—even if some things just happen without being determined by causes that were there in advance—it would still be very significant if everything *we did* were determined before we did it. However free you might feel when choosing between fruit and cake, or between two candidates in an election, you would really be able to make only one choice in those circumstances—though if the circumstances or your desires had been different, you would have chosen differently.

If you believed that about yourself and other people, it would probably change the way you felt about things. For instance, could you blame yourself for giving in to temptation and having the cake? Would it make sense to say, "I really should have had a peach instead," if you *couldn't* have chosen a peach instead? It certainly wouldn't make sense to say it if there *was* no fruit. So how can it make sense if there *was* fruit, but you couldn't have chosen it because it was determined in advance that you would choose cake?

This seems to have serious consequences. Besides not being able sensibly to blame yourself for having had cake, you probably wouldn't be able sensibly to blame anyone at all for doing something bad, or praise them for doing something good. If it was determined in advance that they would do it, it was inevitable: they couldn't have done anything else, given the circumstances as they were. So how can we hold them responsible?

You may be very mad at someone who comes to a party at your house and steals all your Glenn Gould records, but suppose you believed that his action was determined in advance by his nature and the situation. Suppose you believed that everything he did, including the earlier actions that had contributed to the formation of his character, was determined in advance by earlier circumstances. Could you still hold him responsible for such low-grade behavior? Or would it be more reasonable to regard him as a kind of natural disaster—as if your records had been eaten by termites?

People disagree about this. Some think that if determinism is true, no one can reasonably be praised or blamed for anything, any more than the rain can be praised or blamed for falling. Others think that it still makes sense to praise good actions and condemn bad ones, even if they were inevitable. After all, the fact that someone was determined in advance to behave badly doesn't mean that he *didn't* behave badly. If he steals your records, that shows inconsiderateness and dishonesty, whether it was determined or not. Furthermore, if we don't blame him, or perhaps even punish him, he'll probably do it again.

On the other hand, if we think that what he did was determined in advance, this seems more like punishing a dog for chewing on the rug. It doesn't mean we hold him responsible for what he did: we're just trying to influence his behavior in the future. I myself don't think it makes sense to blame someone for doing what it was impossible for him not to do. (Though of course determinism implies that it was determined in advance that I would think this.)

These are the problems we must face if determinism is true. But perhaps it isn't true. Many scientists now believe that it isn't true for the basic particles of matter—that in a given situation, there's more than one thing that an electron may do. Perhaps if determinism isn't true for human actions, either, this leaves room for free will and responsibility. What if human actions, or at least some of them, are not determined in advance? What if, up to the moment when you choose, it's an open possibility that you will choose either chocolate cake or a peach? Then, so far as what has happened before is concerned, you *could* choose either one. Even if you actually choose cake, you could have chosen a peach.

But is even this enough for free will? Is this all you mean when you say, "I could have chosen fruit instead?"—that the choice wasn't determined in advance? No, you believe something more. You believe that *you* determined what you would do, by *doing* it. It wasn't determined in advance, but it didn't *just happen*, either. *You did it*, and you could have done the opposite. But what does that mean?

This is a funny question: we all know what it means to *do* something. But the problem is, if the act wasn't determined in advance, by your desires, beliefs, and personality, among other

[55]

things, it seems to be something that just happened, without any explanation. And in that case, how was it *your doing*?

One possible reply would be that there is no answer to that question. Free action is just a basic feature of the world, and it can't be analyzed. There's a difference between something just happening without a cause and an action just being *done* without a cause. It's a difference we all understand, even if we can't explain it.

Some people would leave it at that. But others find it suspicious that we must appeal to this unexplained idea to explain the sense in which you could have chosen fruit instead of cake. Up to now it has seemed that determinism is the big threat to responsibility. But now it seems that even if our choices are not determined in advance, it is still hard to understand in what way we *can* do what we don't do. Either of two choices may be possible in advance, but unless I determine which of them occurs, it is no more my responsibility than if it was determined by causes beyond my control. And how can *I* determine it if *nothing* determines it?

This raises the alarming possibility that we're not responsible for our actions whether determinism is true *or* whether it's false. If determinism is true, antecedent circumstances are responsible. If determinism is false, nothing is responsible. That would really be a dead end.

There is another possible view, completely opposite to most of what we've been saying. Some people think responsibility for our actions *requires* that our actions be determined, rather than requiring that they not be. The claim is that for an action to be something you have done, it has to be produced by certain kinds of causes in you. For instance, when you chose the chocolate cake, that was something you did, rather than something that just happened, because you wanted chocolate cake more than you wanted a peach. Because your appetite for cake was stronger at the time than your desire to avoid gaining weight, it resulted in your choosing the cake. In other cases of action, the psychological explanation will be more complex, but there will always be one—otherwise the action wouldn't be yours. This explanation seems to mean that what you did was determined in advance after all. If it wasn't determined by anything, it was just an unexplained event, something that happened out of the blue rather than something that you did.

According to this position, causal determination by itself does not threaten freedom—only a certain *kind* of cause does that. If you grabbed the cake because someone else pushed you into it, then it wouldn't be a free choice. But free action doesn't require that there be no determining cause at all: it means that the cause has to be of a familiar psychological type.

I myself can't accept this solution. If I thought that everything I did was determined by my circumstances and my psychological condition, I would feel trapped. And if I thought the same about everybody else, I would feel that they were like a lot of puppets. It wouldn't make sense to hold them responsible for their actions any more than you hold a dog or a cat or even an elevator responsible.

On the other hand, I'm not sure I understand how responsibility for our choices makes sense if they are *not* determined. It's not clear what it means to say *I* determine the choice, if nothing about me determines it. So perhaps the feeling that you could have chosen a peach instead of a piece of cake is a philosophical illusion, and couldn't be right whatever was the case.

To avoid this conclusion, you would have to explain (a) what you *mean* if you say you could have done something other than what you did, and (b) what you and the world would have to be like for this to be true.

7

Right and Wrong

Suppose you work in a library, checking people's books as they leave, and a friend asks you to let him smuggle out a hard-to-find reference work that he wants to own.

You might hesitate to agree for various reasons. You might be afraid that he'll be caught, and that both you and he will then get into trouble. You might want the book to stay in the library so that you can consult it yourself.

But you may also think that what he proposes is wrong—that he shouldn't do it and you shouldn't help him. If you think that, what does it mean, and what, if anything, makes it true?

To say it's wrong is not just to say it's against the rules. There can be bad rules which prohibit what isn't wrong—like a law against criticizing the government. A rule can also be bad because it requires something that *is* wrong—like a law that requires racial segregation in hotels and restaurants. The ideas of wrong and right are different from the ideas of what is and is not against the rules. Otherwise they couldn't be used in the evaluation of rules as well as of actions.

If you think it would be wrong to help your friend steal the book, then you will feel uncomfortable about doing it: in some way you won't want to do it, even if you are also reluctant to refuse help to a friend. Where does the desire not to do it come from; what is its motive, the reason behind it?

There are various ways in which something can be wrong, but in this case, if you had to explain it, you'd probably say that it would be unfair to other users of the library who may be just as interested in the book as your friend is, but who consult it in the reference room, where anyone who needs it can find it. You may also feel that to let him take it would betray your employers, who are paying you precisely to keep this sort of thing from happening.

These thoughts have to do with effects on others—not necessarily effects on their feelings, since they may never find out about it, but some kind of damage nevertheless. In general, the thought that something is wrong depends on its impact not just on the person who does it but on other people. They wouldn't like it, and they'd object if they found out.

But suppose you try to explain all this to your friend, and he says, "I know the head librarian wouldn't like it if he found out, and probably some of the other users of the library would be unhappy to find the book gone, but who cares? I want the book; why should I care about them?"

The argument that it would be wrong is supposed to give him a reason not to do it. But if someone just doesn't care about other people, what reason does he have to refrain from doing any of the things usually thought to be wrong, if he can get away with it: what reason does he have not to kill, steal, lie, or hurt others? If he can get what he wants by doing such things, why shouldn't he? And if there's no reason why he shouldn't, in what sense is it wrong?

Of course most people do care about others to some extent. But if someone doesn't care, most of us wouldn't conclude that he's exempt from morality. A person who kills someone just to steal his wallet, without caring about the victim, is not automatically excused. The fact that he doesn't care doesn't make it all right: He *should* care. But *why* should he care?

There have been many attempts to answer this

question. One type of answer tries to identify something else that the person already cares about, and then connect morality to it.

For example, some people believe that even if you can get away with awful crimes on this earth, and are not punished by the law or your fellow men, such acts are forbidden by God, who will punish you after death (and reward you if you didn't do wrong when you were tempted to). So even when it seems to be in your interest to do such a thing, it really isn't. Some people have even believed that if there is no God to back up moral requirements with the threat of punishment and the promise of reward, morality is an illusion: "If God does not exist, everything is permitted."

This is a rather crude version of the religious foundation for morality. A more appealing version might be that the motive for obeying God's commands is not fear but love. He loves you, and you should love Him, and should wish to obey His commands in order not to offend Him.

But however we interpret the religious motivation, there are three objections to this type of answer. First, plenty of people who don't believe in God still make judgments of right and wrong, and think no one should kill another for his wallet even if he can be sure to get away with it. Second, if God exists, and forbids what's wrong, that still isn't what *makes* it wrong. Murder is wrong in itself, and that's *why* God forbids it (if He does.) God couldn't make just any old thing wrong—like putting on your left sock before your right—simply by prohibiting it. If God would punish you for doing that it would be inadvisable to do it, but it wouldn't be wrong. Third, fear of punishment and hope of reward, and even love of God, seem not to be the right motives for morality. If you think it's wrong to kill, cheat, or steal, you should want to avoid doing such things because they are bad things to do to the victims, not just because you fear the consequences for yourself, or because you don't want to offend your Creator.

This third objection also applies to other explanations of the force of morality which appeal to the interests of the person who must act. For example, it may be said that you should treat others with consideration so that they'll do the same for you. This may be sound advice, but it is valid only so far as you think what you do will affect how others treat you. It's not a reason for doing the right thing if others won't find out about it, or against doing the wrong thing if you can get away with it (like being a hit and run driver).

There is no substitute for a direct concern for other people as the basis of morality. But morality is supposed to apply to everyone: and can we assume that everyone has such a concern for others? Obviously not: some people are very selfish, and even those who are not selfish may care only about the people they know, and not about everyone. So where will we find a reason that everyone has not to hurt other people, even those they don't know?

Well, there's one general argument against hurting other people which can be given to anybody who understands English (or any other language), and which seems to show that he has *some* reason to care about others, even if in the end his selfish motives are so strong that he persists in treating other people badly anyway. It's an argument that I'm sure you've heard, and it goes like this: "How would you like it if someone did that to you?"

It's not easy to explain how this argument is supposed to work. Suppose you're about to steal someone else's umbrella as you leave a restaurant in a rainstorm, and a bystander says, "How would you like it if someone did that to you?" Why is it supposed to make you hesitate, or feel guilty?

Obviously the direct answer to the question is supposed to be, "I wouldn't like it at all!" But what's the next step? Suppose you were to say, "I wouldn't like it if someone did that to me. But luckily no one *is* doing it to me. I'm doing it to someone else, and I don't mind that at all!"

This answer misses the point of the question. When you are asked how you would like it if someone did that to you, you are supposed to think about all the feelings you would have if someone stole your umbrella. And that includes more than just "not liking it"—as you wouldn't "like it" if you stubbed your toe on a rock. If someone stole your umbrella you'd *resent* it. You'd have feelings about the umbrella thief, not just about the loss of the umbrella. You'd think, "Where does he get off, taking my umbrella that I bought with my hard-earned money and that I had the foresight to bring after reading the weather report? Why didn't he bring his own umbrella?" and so forth.

When our own interests are threatened by the inconsiderate behavior of others, most of us find it easy to appreciate that those others have a reason to be more considerate. When you are hurt, you probably feel that other people should care about it: you don't think it's no concern of theirs, and that they have no reason to avoid hurting you. That is the feeling that the "How would you like it?" argument is supposed to arouse.

Because if you admit that you would *resent* it if someone else did to you what you are now

[65]

doing to him, you are admitting that you think he would have a reason not to do it to you. And if you admit that, you have to consider what that reason is. It couldn't be just that it's *you* that he's hurting, of all the people in the world. There's no special reason for him not to steal *your* umbrella, as opposed to anyone else's. There's nothing so special about you. Whatever the reason is, it's a reason he would have against hurting anyone else in the same way. And it's a reason anyone else would have too, in a similar situation, against hurting you or anyone else.

But if it's a reason anyone would have not to hurt anyone else in this way, then it's a reason *you* have not to hurt someone else in this way (since *anyone* means *everyone*). Therefore it's a reason not to steal the other person's umbrella now.

This is a matter of simple consistency. Once you admit that another person would have a reason not to harm you in similar circumstances, and once you admit that the reason he would have is very general and doesn't apply only to you, or to him, then to be consistent you have to admit that the same reason applies to you now. You shouldn't steal the umbrella, and you ought to feel guilty if you do.

Someone could escape from this argument if, when he was asked, "How would you like it if someone did that to you?" he answered, "I wouldn't resent it at all. I wouldn't *like* it if someone stole my umbrella in a rainstorm, but I wouldn't think there was any reason for him to consider my feelings about it." But how many people could honestly give that answer? I think most people, unless they're crazy, would think that their own interests and harms matter, not only to themselves, but in a way that gives other people a reason to care about them too. We all think that when we suffer it is not just bad *for us*, but *bad, period.*

The basis of morality is a belief that good and harm to particular people (or animals) is good or bad not just from their point of view, but from a more general point of view, which every thinking person can understand. That means that each person has a reason to consider not only his own interests but the interests of others in deciding what to do. And it isn't enough if he is considerate only of some others—his family and friends, those he specially cares about. Of course he will care more about certain people, and also about himself. But he has some reason to consider the effect of what he does on the good or harm of everyone. If he's like most of us, that is what he thinks others should do with regard to him, even if they aren't friends of his.

» «

Even if this is right, it is only a bare outline of the source of morality. It doesn't tell us in detail how we should consider the interests of others, or how we should weigh them against the special interest we all have in ourselves and the particular people close to us. It doesn't even tell us how much we should care about people in other countries in comparison with our fellow citizens. There are many disagreements among those who accept morality in general, about what in particular is right and what is wrong.

For instance: should you care about every other person as much as you care about yourself? Should you in other words love your neighbor as yourself (even if he isn't your neighbor)? Should you ask yourself, every time you go to a movie, whether the cost of the ticket could provide more happiness if you gave it to someone else, or donated the money to famine relief?

Very few people are so unselfish. And if someone were that impartial between himself and others, he would probably also feel that he should be just as impartial *among* other people. That would rule out caring more about his friends and relatives than he does about strangers. He might have special feelings about certain people who are close to him, but complete impartiality would mean that he won't *favor* them—if for example he has to choose between helping a friend or a stranger to avoid suffering, or between taking his children to a movie and donating the money to famine relief.

This degree of impartiality seems too much to ask of most people: someone who had it would be a kind of terrifying saint. But it's an important question in moral thought, how much impartiality we should try for. You are a particular person, but you are also able to recognize that you're just one person among many others, and no more important than they are, when looked at from outside. How much should that point of view influence you? You do matter somewhat from outside—otherwise you wouldn't think other people had any reason to care about what they did to you. But you don't matter as much from the outside as you matter to yourself, from the inside—since from the outside you don't matter any more than anybody else.

Not only is it unclear how impartial we should be; it's unclear what would make an answer to this question the right one. Is there a single correct way for everyone to strike the balance between what he cares about personally and what matters impartially? Or will the answer vary from person to person depending on the strength of their different motives?

This brings us to another big issue: Are right and wrong the same for everyone?

Morality is often thought to be universal. If something is wrong, it's supposed to be wrong for everybody; for instance if it's wrong to kill someone because you want to steal his wallet, then it's wrong whether you care about him or not. But if something's being wrong is supposed to be a reason against doing it, and if your reasons for doing things depend on your motives and people's motives can vary greatly, then it looks as though there won't be a single right and wrong for everybody. There won't be a single right and wrong, because if people's basic motives differ, there won't be one basic standard of behavior that everyone has a reason to follow.

There are three ways of dealing with this problem, none of them very satisfactory.

First, we could say that the same things *are* right and wrong for everybody, but that not everyone has a reason to do what's right and avoid what's wrong: only people with the right sort of "moral" motives—particularly a concern for others—have any reason to do what's right, for its own sake. This makes morality universal, but at the cost of draining it of its force. It's not clear what it amounts to to say that it would be wrong for someone to commit murder, but he has no reason not to do it.

Second, we could say that everyone has a reason to do what's right and avoid what's wrong, but that these reasons don't depend on people's actual motives. Rather they are reasons to change our motives if they aren't the right ones. This connects morality with reasons for action, but leaves it unclear what these universal reasons are which do not depend on motives that everyone actually has. What does it mean to say that a murderer had a reason not to do it, even though none of his actual motives or desires gave him such a reason?

Third, we could say that morality is not universal, and that what a person is morally required to do goes only as far as what he has a certain kind of reason to do, where the reason depends on how much he actually cares about other people in general. If he has strong moral motives, they will yield strong reasons and strong moral requirements. If his moral motives are weak or nonexistent, the moral requirements on him will likewise be weak or nonexistent. This may seem psychologically realistic, but it goes against the idea that the same moral rules apply to all of us, and not only to good people.

The question whether moral requirements are universal comes up not only when we compare the motives of different individuals, but also when we compare the moral standards that are accepted in different societies and at different times. Many things that you probably think are wrong have been accepted as morally correct by large groups of people in the past: slavery, serfdom, human sacrifice, racial segregation, denial of religious and political freedom, hereditary

[71]

caste systems. And probably some things you now think are right will be thought wrong by future societies. Is it reasonable to believe that there is some single truth about all this, even though we can't be sure what it is? Or is it more reasonable to believe that right and wrong are relative to a particular time and place and social background?

There is one way in which right and wrong are obviously relative to circumstances. It is usually right to return a knife you have borrowed to its owner if he asks for it back. But if he has gone crazy in the meantime, and wants the knife to murder someone with, then you shouldn't return it. This isn't the kind of relativity I am talking about, because it doesn't mean morality is relative at the basic level. It means only that the same basic moral principles will require different actions in different circumstances.

The deeper kind of relativity, which some people believe in, would mean that the most basic standards of right and wrong—like when it is and is not all right to kill, or what sacrifices you're required to make for others—depend entirely on what standards are generally accepted in the society in which you live.

This I find very hard to believe, mainly because it always seems possible to criticize the accepted standards of your own society and say that they are morally mistaken. But if you do that, you must be appealing to some more objective standard, an idea of what is *really* right and wrong, as opposed to what most people think. It is hard to say what this is, but it is an idea most of us understand, unless we are slavish followers of what the community says.

There are many philosophical problems about the content of morality—how a moral concern or respect for others should express itself; whether we should help them get what they want or mainly refrain from harming and hindering them; how impartial we should be, and in what ways. I have left most of these questions aside because my concern here is with the foundation of morality in general—how universal and objective it is.

I should answer one possible objection to the whole idea of morality. You've probably heard it said that the only reason anybody ever does anything is that it makes him feel good, or that not doing it will make him feel bad. If we are really motivated only by our own comfort, it is hopeless for morality to try to appeal to a concern for others. On this view, even apparently moral conduct in which one person seems to sacrifice his own interests for the sake of others is really motivated by his concern for himself: he wants to avoid the guilt he'll feel if he doesn't do the "right" thing, or to experience the warm glow of self-congratulation he'll get if he does. But those who don't have these feelings have no motive to be "moral."

Now it's true that when people do what they think they ought to do, they often feel good about it: similarly if they do what they think is wrong, they often feel bad. But that doesn't mean that these feelings are their motives for acting. In many cases the feelings result from motives which also produce the action. You wouldn't feel good about doing the right thing unless you thought there was some other reason to do it, besides the fact that it would make you feel good. And you wouldn't feel guilty about doing the wrong thing unless you thought that there was some other reason not to do it, besides the fact that it made you feel guilty: something which made it *right* to feel guilty. At least that's how things should be. It's true that some people feel irrational guilt about things they don't have any independent reason to think are wrong—but that's not the way morality is supposed to work.

In a sense, people do what they want to do. But their reasons and motives for wanting to do things vary enormously. I may "want" to give someone my wallet only because he has a gun pointed at my head and threatens to kill me if I don't. And I may want to jump into an icy river to save a drowning stranger not because it will make me feel good, but because I recognize that his life is important, just as mine is, and I recognize that I have a reason to save his life just as he would have a reason to save mine if our positions were reversed.

Moral argument tries to appeal to a capacity for impartial motivation which is supposed to be present in all of us. Unfortunately it may be deeply buried, and in some cases it may not be present at all. In any case it has to compete with powerful selfish motives, and other personal motives that may not be so selfish, in its bid for control of our behavior. The difficulty of justifying morality is not that there is only one human motive, but that there are so many.

8

Justice

Is it unfair that some people are born rich and some are born poor? If it's unfair, should anything be done about it?

The world is full of inequalities—within countries, and from one country to another. Some children are born into comfortable, prosperous homes, and grow up well fed and well educated. Others are born poor, don't get enough to eat, and never have access to much education or medical care. Clearly, this is a matter of luck: we are not responsible for the social or economic class or country into which we are born. The question is, how bad are inequalities which are not the fault of the people who suffer from them? Should governments use their power to try to reduce inequalities of this kind, for which the victims are not responsible?

Some inequalities are deliberately imposed. Racial discrimination, for example, deliberately excludes people of one race from jobs, housing, and education which are available to people of another race. Or women may be kept out of jobs or denied privileges available only to men. This is not merely a matter of bad luck. Racial and sexual discrimination are clearly unfair: they are forms of inequality caused by factors that should not be allowed to influence people's basic welfare. Fairness requires that opportunities should be open to those who are qualified, and it is clearly a good thing when governments try to enforce such equality of opportunity.

But it is harder to know what to say about inequalities that arise in the ordinary course of events, without deliberate racial or sexual discrimination. Because even if there is equality of opportunity, and any qualified person can go to a university or get a job or buy a house or run for office—regardless of race, religion, sex, or national origin—there will still be plenty of inequalities left. People from wealthier backgrounds will usually have better training and more resources, and they will tend to be better able to compete for good jobs. Even in a system of equality of opportunity, some people will have a head start and will end up with greater benefits than others whose native talents are the same.

Not only that, but differences in native talent will produce big differences in the resulting benefits, in a competitive system. Those who have abilities that are in high demand will be able to earn much more than those without any special skills or talents. These differences too are partly a matter of luck. Though people have to develop and use their abilities, no amount of effort would enable most people to act like Meryl Streep, paint like Picasso, or manufacture automobiles like Henry Ford. Something similar is true of lesser accomplishments. The luck of both natural talent and family and class background are important factors in determining one's income and position in a competitive society. Equal opportunity produces unequal results.

These inequalities, unlike the results of racial and sexual discrimination, are produced by choices and actions that don't seem wrong in themselves. People try to provide for their children and give them a good education, and some have more money to use for this purpose than others. People pay for the products, services, and performances they want, and some performers or manufacturers get richer than others because what they have to offer is wanted by more people. Businesses and organizations of all kinds try to hire employees who will do the job well, and pay higher salaries for those with unusual skills. If one restaurant is full of people and another next door is empty because the first has a talented chef and the second doesn't, the customers who choose the first restaurant and avoid the second haven't done anything wrong, even though their choices have an unhappy effect on the owner and employees of the second restaurant, and on their families.

Such effects are most disturbing when they leave some people in a very bad way. In some countries large segments of the population live in poverty from generation to generation. But even in a wealthy country like the United States, lots of people start life with two strikes against them, from economic and educational disadvantages. Some can overcome those disadvantages, but it's much harder than making good from a higher starting point.

Most disturbing of all are the enormous inequalities in wealth, health, education, and development between rich and poor countries. Most people in the world have no chance of ever being as well off economically as the poorest people in Europe, Japan, or the United States. These large differences in good and bad luck certainly seem unfair; but what, if anything, should be done about them?

We have to think about both the inequality itself, and the remedy that would be needed to reduce or get rid of it. The main question about the inequalities themselves is: What kinds of *causes* of inequality are wrong? The main question about remedies is: What *methods* of interfering with the inequality are right?

In the case of deliberate racial or sexual discrimination, the answers are easy. The cause of the inequality is wrong because the discriminator is *doing* something wrong. And the remedy is simply to prevent him from doing it. If a landlord refuses to rent to blacks, he should be prosecuted.

But the questions are more difficult in other cases. The problem is that inequalities which seem wrong can arise from causes which don't involve people *doing* anything wrong. It seems unfair that people born much poorer than others should suffer disadvantages through no fault of their own. But such inequalities exist because some people have been more successful than others at earning money and have tried to help their children as much as possible; and because people tend to marry members of their own economic and social class, wealth and position accumulate and are passed on from generation to generation. The actions which combine to form these causes—employment decisions, purchases, marriages, bequests, and efforts to provide for and educate children, don't seem wrong in themselves. What's wrong, if anything, is the result: that some people start life with undeserved disadvantages.

If we object to this kind of bad luck as unfair, it must be because we object to people's suffering disadvantages through no fault of their own, merely as a result of the ordinary operation of the socioeconomic system into which they are born. Some of us may also believe that all bad luck that is not a person's fault, such as that of being born with a physical handicap, should be compensated if possible. But let us leave those cases aside in this discussion. I want to concentrate on the undeserved inequalities that arise through the working of society and the economy, particularly a competitive economy.

The two main sources of these undeserved inequalities, as I have said, are differences in the socioeconomic classes into which people are born, and differences in their natural abilities or talents for tasks which are in demand. You may not think there is anything wrong with inequality caused in these ways. But if you think there is something wrong with it, and if you think a society should try to reduce it, then you must propose a remedy which either interferes with the causes themselves, or interferes with the unequal effects directly.

Now the causes themselves, as we have seen, include relatively innocent choices by many people about how to spend their time and money and how to lead their lives. To interfere with people's choices about what products to buy, how to help their children, or how much to pay their employees, is very different from interfering with them when they want to rob banks or discriminate against blacks or women. A more indirect interference in the economic life of individuals is taxation, particularly taxation of income and inheritance, and some taxes on consumption, which can be designed to take more from the rich than from the poor. This is one way a government can try to reduce the development of great inequalities in wealth over generations—by not letting people keep all of their money.

More important, however, would be to use the public resources obtained through taxes to provide some of the missing advantages of education and support to the children of those families that can't afford to do it themselves. Public social welfare programs try to do this, by using tax revenues to provide basic benefits of health care, food, housing, and education. This attacks the inequalities directly.

When it comes to the inequalities that result from differences in ability, there isn't much one can do to interfere with the causes short of abolishing the competitive economy. So long as there is competition to hire people for jobs, competition between people to get jobs, and competition between firms for customers, some people are going to make more money than others. The only alternative would be a centrally directed economy in which everyone was paid roughly the same and people were assigned to their jobs by some kind of centralized authority. Though it has been tried, this system has heavy costs in both freedom and efficiency—far too heavy, in my opinion, to be acceptable, though others would disagree.

If one wants to reduce the inequalities resulting from different abilities without getting rid of the competitive economy, it will be necessary to attack the inequalities themselves. This can be done through higher taxation of higher incomes, and some free provision of public services to everyone, or to people with lower incomes. It could include cash payments to those whose earning power is lowest, in the form of a so-called "negative income tax." None of these programs would get rid of undeserved inequalities completely, and any system of taxation will have other effects on the economy, including effects on employment and the poor, which may be hard to predict; so the issue of a remedy is always complicated.

But to concentrate on the philosophical point: the measures needed to reduce undeserved inequalities arising from differences in class background and natural talent will involve interference with people's economic activities, mainly through taxation: the government takes money from some people and uses it to help others. This is not the only use of taxation, or even the main use: many taxes are spent on things which benefit the well-off more than the poor. But *redistributive* taxation, as it is called, is the type relevant to our problem. It does involve the use of government power to interfere with what people do, not because what they do is wrong in itself, like theft or discrimination, but because it contributes to an effect which seems unfair.

There are those who don't think redistributive taxation is right, because the government shouldn't interfere with people unless they are doing something wrong, and the economic transactions that produce all these inequalities aren't wrong, but perfectly innocent. They may also hold that there's nothing wrong with the resulting inequalities themselves: that even though they're *undeserved* and not the fault of the victims, society is not obliged to fix them. That's just life, they will say: some people are more fortunate than others. The only time we have to *do* anything about it is when the misfortune is the result of someone's doing a wrong to someone else.

This is a controversial political issue, and there are many different opinions about it. Some people object more to the inequalities that come from the socioeconomic class a person is born into, than to the inequalities resulting from differences in talent or ability. They don't like the effects of one person being born rich and another in a slum, but feel that a person deserves what he can earn with his own efforts— so that there's nothing unfair about one person earning a lot and another very little because the first has a marketable talent or capacity for learning sophisticated skills while the second can only do unskilled labor.

I myself think that inequalities resulting from either of these causes are unfair, and that it is clearly unjust when a socioeconomic system results in some people living under significant material and social disadvantages through no fault of their own, if this could be prevented through a system of redistributive taxation and social welfare programs. But to make up your own mind about the issue, you have to consider both what causes of inequality you find unfair, and what remedies you find legitimate.

We've been talking mainly about the problem of social justice within one society. The problem is much more difficult on a world scale, both because the inequalities are so great and because it's not clear what remedies are possible in the absence of a world government that could levy world taxes and see that they are used effectively. There is no prospect of a world government, which is just as well, since it would probably be a horrible government in many ways. However there is still a problem of global justice, though it's hard to know what to do about it in the system of separate sovereign states we have now.

9

Death

Everybody dies, but not everybody agrees about what death is. Some believe they will survive after the death of their bodies, going to Heaven or Hell or somewhere else, becoming a ghost, or returning to Earth in a different body, perhaps not even as a human being. Others believe they will cease to exist—that the self is snuffed out when the body dies. And among those who believe they will cease to exist, some think this is a terrible fact, and others don't.

It is sometimes said that no one can conceive of his own nonexistence, and that therefore we can't really believe that our existence will come to an end with our deaths. But this doesn't seem true. Of course you can't conceive of your own nonexistence *from the inside*. You can't conceive of what it would be like to be totally annihilated, because there's nothing it would be like, from the inside. But in that sense, you can't conceive of what it would be like to be completely unconscious, even temporarily. The fact that you can't conceive of that from the inside doesn't mean you can't conceive of it at all: you just have to think of yourself from the outside, having been knocked out, or in a deep sleep. And even though you have to be conscious to *think* that, it doesn't mean that you're thinking *of* yourself as conscious.

It's the same with death. To imagine your own annihilation you have to think of it from the outside—think about the body of the person you are, with all the life and experience gone from it. To imagine something it is not necessary to imagine how it would feel for *you* to experience it. When you imagine your own funeral, you are not imagining the impossible situation of being *present* at your own funeral: you're imagining how it would look through someone else's eyes. Of course you are alive while you think of your own death, but that is no more of a problem than being conscious while imagining yourself unconscious.

The question of survival after death is related to the mind-body problem, which we discussed earlier. If dualism is true, and each person con-

sists of a soul and a body connected together, we
can understand how life after death might be
possible. The soul would have to be able to exist
on its own and have a mental life without the
help of the body: then it might leave the body
when the body dies, instead of being destroyed.
It wouldn't be able to have the kind of mental
life of action and sensory perception that depends on being attached to the body (unless it
got attached to a new body), but it might have a
different sort of inner life, perhaps depending
on different causes and influences—direct com-
munication with other souls, for instance.

I say life after death *might* be possible if dualism were true. It also might not be possible, because the survival of the soul, and its continued
consciousness, might depend entirely on the
support and stimulation it gets from the body in
which it is housed—and it might not be able to
switch bodies.

But if dualism is not true, and mental processes go on in the brain and are entirely depen-
dent on the biological functioning of the brain
and the rest of the organism, then life after
death of the body is not possible. Or to put it
more exactly, mental life after death would require the restoration of biological, physical life:
it would require that the *body* come to life again.
This might become technically possible some

day: It may become possible to freeze people's bodies when they die, and then later on by advanced medical procedures to fix whatever was the matter with them, and bring them back to life.

Even if this became possible, there would still be a question whether the person who was brought to life several centuries later would be you or somebody else. Maybe if you were frozen after death and your body was later revived, *you* wouldn't wake up, but only someone very like you, with memories of your past life. But even if revival after death of the same you in the same body should become possible, that's not what's ordinarily meant by life after death. Life after death usually means life without your old body.

It's hard to know how we could decide whether we have separable souls. All the evidence is that *before* death, conscious life depends entirely on what happens in the nervous system. If we go only by ordinary observation, rather than religious doctrines or spiritualist claims to communicate with the dead, there is no reason to believe in an afterlife. Is that, however, a reason to believe that there is *not* an afterlife? I think so, but others may prefer to remain neutral.

Still others may believe in an afterlife on the basis of faith, in the absence of evidence. I myself don't fully understand how this kind of faith-inspired belief is possible, but evidently some people can manage it, and even find it natural.

Let me turn to the other part of the problem: how we ought to *feel* about death. Is it a good thing, a bad thing, or neutral? I am talking about how it's reasonable to feel about your own death—not so much about other people's. Should you look forward to the prospect of death · with terror, sorrow, indifference, or relief?

Obviously it depends on what death is. If there is life after death, the prospect will be grim or happy depending on where your soul will end up. But the difficult and most philosophically interesting question is how we should feel about death if it's the end. Is it a terrible thing to go out of existence?

People differ about this. Some say that nonexistence, being nothing at all, can't possibly be either good or bad for the dead person. Others say that to be annihilated, to have the possible future course of your life cut off completely, is the ultimate evil, even if we all have to face it. Still others say death is a blessing—not of course if it comes too early, but eventually—because it would be unbearably boring to live forever.

If death without anything after it is either a

good or a bad thing for the person who dies, it must be a *negative* good or evil. Since in itself it is nothing, it can't be either pleasant or unpleasant. If it's good, that must be because it is the absence of something bad (like boredom or pain); if it's bad, that must be because it is the absence of something good (like interesting or pleasant experiences).

Now it might seem that death can't have any value, positive or negative, because someone who doesn't exist can't be either benefited or harmed: after all, even a *negative* good or evil has to happen to *somebody*. But on reflection, this is not really a problem. We can say that the person who *used* to exist has been benefited or harmed by death. For instance, suppose he is trapped in a burning building, and a beam falls on his head, killing him, instantly. As a result, he doesn't suffer the agony of being burned to death. It seems that in that case we can say he was lucky to be killed painlessly, because it avoided something worse. Death at that time was a negative good, because it saved him from the positive evil he would otherwise have suffered for the next five minutes. And the fact that he's not around to enjoy that negative good doesn't mean it's not a good for him at all. "Him" means the person who was alive, and who would have suffered if he hadn't died.

The same kind of thing could be said about death as a negative evil. When you die, all the good things in your life come to a stop: no more meals, movies, travel, conversation, love, work, books, music, or anything else. If those things would be good, their absence is bad. Of course you won't *miss* them: death is not like being locked up in solitary confinement. But the ending of everything good in life, because of the stopping of life itself, seems clearly to be a negative evil for the person who was alive and is now dead. When someone we know dies, we feel sorry not only for ourselves but for him, because he can't see the sun shine today, or smell the bread in the toaster.

When you think of your own death, the fact that all the good things in life will come to an end is certainly a reason for regret. But that doesn't seem to be the whole story. Most people want there to be more of what they enjoy in life, but for some people, the prospect of nonexistence is itself frightening, in a way that isn't adequately explained by what has been said so far. The thought that the world will go on without you, that you will become *nothing*, is very hard to take in.

It's not clear why. We all accept the fact that there was a time before we were born, when we didn't yet exist—so why should we be so disturbed at the prospect of nonexistence after our death? But somehow it doesn't feel the same. The prospect of nonexistence is frightening, at least to many people, in a way that past nonexistence cannot be.

The fear of death is very puzzling, in a way that regret about the end of life is not. It's easy to understand that we might want to have more life, more of the things it contains, so that we see death as a negative evil. But how can the *prospect* of your own nonexistence be alarming in a positive way? If we really cease to exist at death, there's nothing to look forward to, so how can there be anything to be afraid of? If one thinks about it logically, it seems as though death should be something to be afraid of only if we *will* survive it, and perhaps undergo some terrifying transformation. But that doesn't prevent many people from thinking that annihilation is one of the worst things that could happen to them.

10

The Meaning of Life

Perhaps you have had the thought that nothing really matters, because in two hundred years we'll all be dead. This is a peculiar thought, because it's not clear why the fact that we'll be dead in two hundred years should imply that nothing we do now really matters.

The idea seems to be that we are in some kind of rat race, struggling to achieve our goals and make something of our lives, but that this makes sense only if those achievements will be permanent. But they won't be. Even if you produce a great work of literature which continues to be read thousands of years from now, eventually the solar system will cool or the universe will wind down or collapse, and all trace of your efforts will vanish. In any case, we can't hope for even a fraction of this sort of immortality. If there's any point at all to what we do, we have to find it within our own lives.

Why is there any difficulty in that? You can explain the point of most of the things you do. You work to earn money to support yourself and perhaps your family. You eat because you're hungry, sleep because you're tired, go for a walk or call up a friend because you feel like it, read the newspaper to find out what's going on in the world. If you didn't do any of those things you'd be miserable; so what's the big problem?

The problem is that although there are justifications and explanations for most of the things, big and small, that we do *within* life, none of these explanations explain the point of your life as a whole—the whole of which all these activities, successes and failures, strivings and disappointments are parts. If you think about the whole thing, there seems to be no point to it at all. Looking at it from the outside, it wouldn't matter if you had never existed. And after you have gone out of existence, it won't matter that you did exist.

Of course your existence matters to other people—your parents and others who care about you—but taken as a whole, their lives have no point either, so it ultimately doesn't matter that you matter to them. You matter to them and they matter to you, and that may give your life a feeling of significance, but you're just taking in each other's washing, so to speak. Given that any person exists, he has needs and concerns which make particular things and people within his life matter to him. But the *whole thing* doesn't matter.

But does it matter that it doesn't matter? "So what?" you might say. "It's enough that it matters whether I get to the station before my train leaves, or whether I've remembered to feed the cat. I don't need more than that to keep going." This is a perfectly good reply. But it only works if you really can avoid setting your sights higher, and asking what the point of the whole thing is. For once you do that, you open yourself to the possibility that your life is meaningless.

The thought that you'll be dead in two hundred years is just a way of seeing your life embedded in a larger context, so that the point of smaller things inside it seems not to be enough—seems to leave a larger question unanswered. But what if your life as a whole did have a point in relation to something larger? Would that mean that it wasn't meaningless after all?

There are various ways your life could have a larger meaning. You might be part of a political or social movement which changed the world for the better, to the benefit of future generations. Or you might just help provide a good life for your own children and their descendants. Or your life might be thought to have meaning in a religious context, so that your time on Earth was just a preparation for an eternity in direct contact with God.

About the types of meaning that depend on relations to other people, even people in the distant future, I've already indicated what the problem is. If one's life has a point as a part of something larger, it is still possible to ask about that larger thing, what is the point of *it*? Either there's an answer in terms of something still larger or there isn't. If there is, we simply repeat the question. If there isn't, then our search for a point has come to an end with something which has no point. But if that pointlessness is acceptable for the larger thing of which our life is a part, why shouldn't it be acceptable already for our life taken as a whole? Why isn't it all right for your life to be pointless? And if it isn't acceptable there, why should it be acceptable when we get to the larger context? Why don't we have to go on to ask, "But what is the point of all *that*?" (human history, the succession of the generations, or whatever).

The appeal to a religious meaning to life is a bit different. If you believe that the meaning of your life comes from fulfilling the purpose of God, who loves you, and seeing Him in eternity, then it doesn't seem appropriate to ask, "And what is the point of *that*?" It's supposed to be something which is its own point, and can't have a purpose outside itself. But for this very reason it has its own problems.

The idea of God seems to be the idea of something that can explain everything else, without having to be explained itself. But it's very hard to understand how there could be such a thing. If we ask the question, "Why is the world like this?" and are offered a religious answer, how can we be prevented from asking again, "And why is *that* true?" What kind of answer would bring all of our "Why?" questions to a stop, once and for all? And if they can stop there, why couldn't they have stopped earlier?

The same problem seems to arise if God and His purposes are offered as the ultimate explanation of the value and meaning of our lives. The idea that our lives fulfil God's purpose is supposed to give them their point, in a way that doesn't require or admit of any further point. One isn't supposed to ask "What is the point of God?" any more than one is supposed to ask, "What is the explanation of God?"

But my problem here, as with the role of God as ultimate explanation, is that I'm not sure I understand the idea. Can there really be something which gives point to everything else by encompassing it, but which couldn't have, or need, any point itself? Something whose point can't be questioned from outside because there is no outside?

If God is supposed to give our lives a meaning that we can't understand, it's not much of a consolation. God as ultimate justification, like God as ultimate explanation, may be an incomprehensible answer to a question that we can't get rid of. On the other hand, maybe that's the whole point, and I am just failing to understand religious ideas. Perhaps the belief in God is the belief that the universe is intelligible, but not to us.

Leaving that issue aside, let me return to the smaller-scale dimensions of human life. Even if life as a whole is meaningless, perhaps that's nothing to worry about. Perhaps we can recognize it and just go on as before. The trick is to keep your eyes on what's in front of you, and allow justifications to come to an end inside your life, and inside the lives of others to whom you are connected. If you ever ask yourself the question, "But what's the point of being alive at all?"—leading the particular life of a student or bartender or whatever you happen to be—you'll answer "There's no point. It wouldn't matter if

I didn't exist at all, or if I didn't care about any-thing. But I do. That's all there is to it."

Some people find this attitude perfectly satis-fying. Others find it depressing, though un-avoidable. Part of the problem is that some of us have an incurable tendency to take ourselves se-riously. We want to matter to ourselves "from the outside." If our lives as a whole seem point-less, then a part of us is dissatisfied—the part that is always looking over our shoulders at what we are doing. Many human efforts, particularly those in the service of serious ambitions rather than just comfort and survival, get some of their energy from a sense of importance—a sense that what you are doing is not just important to you, but important in some larger sense: impor-tant, period. If we have to give this up, it may threaten to take the wind out of our sails. If life is not real, life is not earnest, and the grave is its goal, perhaps it's ridiculous to take ourselves so seriously. On the other hand, if we can't help taking ourselves so seriously, perhaps we just have to put up with being ridiculous. Life may be not only meaningless but absurd.